Until Air Itself Is Tinted

poems

Cullen Whisenhunt

Until Air Itself Is Tinted

Cover Image: Lindsay Brantley
Book Design: Rowan Kehn

ISBN: 979-8-9868994-3-5

Turning Plow Press

Table of Contents

Dedication: A Work in Progress

Part 1: An Introduction to Bird Watching.. 1

    An Introduction 3

    In Morning.. 4

    A Graveyard of Geese.. 5

    Of Monotony... 6

    Interruption... 7

    Willow Curtains.. 8

    The Flightpaths of Feral Feathers 9

        I: Turkey and Black Vulture 9

        II: Eastern, Western, and Lilian's Meadowlark 10

        III: Mourning Dove... 11

        IV: American Crow 12

        V: American Robin... 13

        VI: Red-tailed, Red-shouldered, and Cooper's Hawk............ 14

        VII: Great Blue Heron.. 15

        VIII: Canadian Goose.. 16

        IX: House Sparrow... 17

        X: Northern Cardinal 18

        XI: Cedar Waxwing 19

        XII: Northern Mockingbird 20

        XIII: Blue Jay.. 21

        XIV: Barn Swallow 22

        XV: Scissor-tailed Flycatcher 23

    It's like a Metaphor... 24

    one wing at a time... 25

    Junco Just So... 26

    Winter Heron.. 28

    Bird Watching... 29

Interlude 31

    Bird Seed Haiku 33

    reflective tanka.. 36

    chickadee tanka... 37

    String Sequence 38

    Statuary Sequence 39

    Sentinel Sequence.. 40

Oklahoma Skaibun 42
Part 2: Until Air Itself Is Tinted 45
The Trial of Paris 47
Among the Trees 48
A Winter Heat 49
The Screamer 50
Overlooking Freeny 51
Dandelion Morning 52
Descending the Staircase 54
Hello Again, Green 56
Li Po 58
Not Crippled but Broken 59
Another Night in Paradise 60
On the Valero Refinery on Veteran's Boulevard 61
Until Air Itself Is Tinted 62
Mimesis 63
And Back Again 64
For a Lover, at Dusk 65
Revision, June 27 66
Knee Deep in October 67
Learning to Lean 68
Joke 69
A Mild One 70
Meditation 72
University Boulevard 73
Visions of Durant, OK 74
A Grasshopper 77
Just Before the Rain-Out 78
Sun Showers 79
Disillusionment of 10:30 81
In Words and Trees 82
Pastures of Plenty 83
Lost Lake 84
October Rain 86
These Branching Moments 87
Meaningless Harmonies 88
Variations at Night 90

Turtle Island Sticky Note.. 93
Fog Like Flame... 95
Snowmelt... 96
After the Solstice.. 97
Tonight 98
Notes on the Poems.. 99
Acknowledgments.. 101
About the Author 103

In Praise of *Until Air Itself Is Tinted*

In *Until Air Itself Is Tinted*, Cullen Whisenhunt approaches his poems with a photographer's keen eye, drawing into sharp focus everyday details that often go overlooked. In this collection, Whisenhunt creates a rich poetic texture, interwoven with cranes and herons, leafy sidewalks and cypress teeth. Indeed, these are poems we can sink our teeth into, the rich imagery set against a vivid backdrop of birdsong and Oklahoma soul.

–Jessica Isaacs, author of *Deep August*
Oklahoma Book Award, 2015

I've been waiting on this book for a while. I first became acquainted with Cullen's work when he was at Southeastern Oklahoma State University and my Department Chair asked me to read a few of Cullen's poems to see if I saw as much potential as they did. I did. Now that potential has become tangible. I honestly enjoyed his first chapbook, *Among the Trees*, but this book is the real deal. While the book is a trove of excellent poetry, I particularly loved the conversation with Ginsberg in "Visions of Durant, OK" and the narrative bent of "Descending the Staircase," but of course, my favorite was the tribute to Oklahoma kids' baseball, "Just Before the Rain-Out"; short, sweet and damn near perfect. Do not miss this book.

–Ron Wallace, author of *Renegade*
Oklahoma Book Award, 2018

A Work in Progress

for Jeanetta Calhoun Mish

I'm out of words for now,
I think, and that's fine—
fair enough, even. For now
no longer feels like the time
for words, but works.
                       Works
that say more than "thanks,"
but repay one who gave me
my own home, repackaged
as "worth something," where
I could find a world I wished
to share myself with others,
where I could work and play
and read and write and love, love,
love like the one who gave it.

What words could make that love visible?

Part 1: An Introduction to Bird Watching

I found out a good many years back practically all I need to know about my general reader; that is to say, you, I'm afraid. You'll deny it up and down, I fear, but I'm really in no position to take your word for it. You're a great bird-lover...

—J.D. Salinger, *Seymour: an Introduction*

An Introduction

I know
Absolutely nothing
About birds.

I bought a field guide to North American birds
and I still haven't managed to identify one fucking feather.

The birds around my apartment, I know,
are small, and dark, and pointy,
but there seems to be no such designation in the guide.
Only beak types and feathering patterns and seasonal habitats.

It has pecks of pictures of birds
on fence-posts or tree branches, but
there are no fences in my neighborhood,
and all the trees are, like, really tall.

The few birds in flight are surprisingly well-lit and still,
as opposed to the shadow droplets
that dash through the sunlight outside my window,
           nothing but blurs with beaks. Now,

I'm not saying I don't like birds,
I do. But I don't like
not knowing about them.
You can't write what you don't know,
which is why all my bird poems are about obvious birds,
like vultures, sitting nice and still as they sail circular,
or herons, those stand-up guys,
or:
           the cardinal, alighting
           on burnt birch limb

(On a side note, I also know nothing about trees...)

In Morning

8 a.m. and the birds
are out in concert krilling
until the blonde pup
bounds up barking, matchsticks
mass migration from meadowlark,
quail-quick and quiet
underneath straight-line
blue jay and finch wing wind.

Only the redbreast remains,
resting on rusted barbwire
or trusting enough to wait
in low branches
for the opportune time
to bounce away through nothing
but air—whole, free.

A Graveyard of Geese

In this mist
-drunk day dawning,
they bed down
between headstones,
their own heads
buried beneath
their wings,
their own bodies
buried beneath
the heat of being
together.

A few strays paddle
a reflecting pool,
feeding on bread
crumbs of grief
and kindness.

Of Monotony
after CK Williams' "Shock"

Furiously a crane

A neck,
high, tight-throated,
anticipating lips, or showing
pearl of smile and peeling
laughter down from the heavens,
making metaphors of our bodies.

Furiously a crane

Hands keystroking
with fingers like tassels
in a hot wind or a heron
shooting sharp and precise into stillness
to pluck satisfaction without ripples.
Our actions as similes.

Furiously a crane

We, images
in perpetual cycle,
carousel projections flitting
against a whiteboard, dipping birds
wishing for furious wingbeats to propel us up, around, away
from the glass surface where we drink
Again. Again. Again...

Interruption

during Ken Hada's "Winter Comes to El Chaparral"

—Shove your laundry tote
across the floor and it will ruffle
like a flock of crows in flight,

and fearing the worst
from this poem of owls,
I will jerk awake on a nearby bench in time

to catch you separating
whites from colors while whispering
lightly in a timbre higher than

I'd have otherwise expected that
I scared *you*—

Willow Curtains

This April afternoon bakes all
in orange, matching
the scissortail's underwing
as it dips and rises, aerials
around almost aimless,
just beyond touching
but close enough to tease,
and my shutter's not near
fast enough to catch
the initial swoop, nor near
prescient enough to meet it
at the mesh point
where toes ascend
into grabbing perch hold.

Instead, I brush aside
willow curtains
to spy goslings lined up
behind mother goose, waddling
single-file towards pond water.
The gander cuts his eye
my way and snake-necks,
hissing.

The Flightpaths of Feral Feathers

I: Turkey and Black Vulture
Cathartes aura and *Coragyps atratus*

Constantly coasting.

Laid back
like that kid
in a high school
group project
content to merely
pick at the carcass
of a passing grade.

But I can't lie,
there's something
appealing
about how far
above it all
they appear,
riding risers
to impossibly
impractical
heights
that nonetheless
leave them closer
to the sun
than we
can ever dream.

II: Eastern, Western, and Lilian's Meadowlark
Sturnella magna, *Sturnella neglecta*, and *Sturnella lilianae*

It's birds like this
that made "yellow-bellied"
the slur it is.

Despite its tucked-tail
form defying
aerodynamics,
its rear end
slung low like
a wounded dog,
let one
of its beady blacks
catch sight of you
and it'll beat it
so quick
you won't believe.

III: Mourning Dove
Zenaida macroura

Like a Star Wars
spacecraft,
it curves
into a delicious point,
putting me in mind
of a Nabooean
noble ship, regal
and graceful
when on the ground,
then quickly
leaping
into laser-like
lightspeed.

IV: American Crow
Corvus brachyrhynchos

The one we're all aware of,
whose flight's
been crystallized
in a ray-straight
colloquialism, but
whose real-life routes
reveal a rambling
too random to rely on.

V: American Robin
Turdus migratorius

Nondescript
for the most part,
except when it drops
and lands heavy
like a load
of its Latinate.

VI: Red-tailed, Red-shouldered, and Cooper's Hawk
Buteo jamaicensis, Buteo lineatus, and *Accipiter cooperii*

Away
from people
always.

I get it.

VII: Great Blue Heron
Ardea herodias

Frightened
from the shorefront,
it beats its way
into a blue streak.
A lone crew member
kayaking away,
bent-necked, powerful,
flowing over lake top
in fluid flaps.

Stroke.
        Stroke.
                Stroke.

VIII: Canadian Goose
Branta canadensis

Famously v-shaped.

Famously ferocious.

Famously, "violence"
starts with a "v"
and ends with a hiss.

IX: House Sparrow
Passer domesticus

An absolute
explosion
of energy
when launching
and landing,
comes careening
around the corner
only to carom off
in a completely
different direction.

In breeze wind,
watch it buffet
about, bumbling
like a high-speed
butterfly,
more distracted than delicate.

X: Northern Cardinal
Cardinalis cardinalis

A faith flyer, each
wingbeat a leap
into the unknown.

Alternately,
often chasing tail.

XI: Cedar Waxwing
Bombycilla cedrorum

I wouldn't know.
I've never seen them
do anything
but be pretty,

but I imagine
they slide smooth
through the air
like the marbling
of their own
coloration.

XII: Northern Mockingbird
Mimus polyglottos

Erratic,
excepting its ever-effort
to run out
any trespassers,
"mocking"
doesn't nearly do enough
to get across
the militance
of this
motherfucker.

XIII: Blue Jay
Cyanocitta cristata

More mocking than
its *polyglottos* peer,
Jay jumps
from limb to limb,
always just ahead
and jeering.

(Whatever its flightpath,
it's too fast
and unspecific
for my photo-reflexes,
and for that
I will never forgive it.)

XIV: Barn Swallow
Hirundo rustica

Slicing
in sleek arcs,
this blade bird
seems one of few
who flies for fun.

It dives
from dugout nest
then turns
directly
into torque and joy.

XV: Scissor-tailed Flycatcher
Tyrannus forficatus

Bird Baryshnikovs
cartwheeling
and cavorting
through Oklahoma
breeze, advancing
via aerials
crossing
dance and gymnastics.

Harbingers of spring,
unquestioned,
unquestionable.

They tailslide.
They stall turn.
They stunt loop
outside,
       inside,
and aileron roll
away.

Some 20-odd
turkey vultures
circle silent
and lazy-like
over the new
elementary.

The kettle wheels
through a soft grey
Oklahoma
winter morning,
northbound toward
the high school building.

Then, on to the
university.

It's like a Metaphor

The melt starts
at midday, dripping
a tempo sharp

as a heater hums
life through the hall.
The silence

of snowbanks thaws
into sparrow song and the crisp
of cardinals

on untouched powder.
These house finches share
the semblance to flame

along the fencerow—
the world warming itself
one wing at a time

Junco Just So

What to do
with you,
waiting
up there
in December
dogwood
branches
bare but
for buds not
yet
set for
blooming?

You dark-eyed
drupe
hung high,
hopeful
though
full-exposed
by leafless
locale,
lend me
no small smatter
of your
confidence
quiet
and unassumed
as your coat
of few colors,
and those
the most
muted.

Your feathers,
no less
smooth
than your wax-
winged brethren

but without
the need
to announce
themselves
in out-
shining light,
whisper back,
shushing:

"No.
You need
not
from me;
only be
as you
are
—just so."

Winter Heron

Among cypress teeth
you stalk, plunging
your whole
head, neck, beak
beneath the cold
surface of a February
freeze.

Your pond-wet
eye glimmers
a survivor's desperation.

Bird Watching

A kidney bean of starlings
floats over a crumbling
schoolhouse, stops
suddenly, elongates upwards
like an arm made
entirely of freckles, stretch
-ing for attention. A bubble
of oblivious pinches off like
meiosis and blows on south
unnoticing.

Later, a decapitated vulture
carcass, rolled by a semi tire,
one elbow pinioned beneath,
wings a feathered acknowledge
-ment in my direction, its down
still wet with blood. I slide my car
just right and do not even think
to wave back.

Interlude
Tanshi

Bird Seed Haiku

lake's edge reflects near-noon
—a bright spot wades in

autumn sunrise
settles on sycamore
half-stripped—surprise!

kite whips in wind
seabirds swing, sway, circle
—who holds the string?

fingertip
pressed to book-spine
—heartbeat

my mother's pitcher:
full of tea stains and memories

pumpkin pie sunrise
purpled by the day after
sleepiness

a bitter wind
blows loose last leaves
—exposing thorns

buzzard circles
over city cemetery
—seems redundant

in every littlebig town
in Oklahoma:
stairs going nowhere

Talihina, November:
shopgirl behind glass
painted porcelain-still

autumn afternoon:
chilly but for the burning
Chinese Pistache

35 seats
face the board, waiting
in the dark

mid-winter:
birdsong softens lifeless limbs

this flurry
is too much for reindeer
frozen in surprise

the last days of spring:
cottonwood snowdrifts
swept away by warming breeze

morning rain
—stars distilled
as droplets in fir trees

poetry scattered
across this page like bird seed
on worn walkways

reflective tanka

Through the doorway,
old man with windows behind—
he walks from the frame,
leaving his shadow
                  behind

chickadee tanka

after Bryan Dahlvang

a statue with seeds
in hand, excited
at the possibility
—chickadees landing
soft as snowflakes

String Sequence

after Irmgard Geul

String theory loses
my mind, but the forest I
remember. I unify
this matter into
distinct lines, flat planes,

design my childhood
along string stretched taut,
my thoughts tied like light
lancing through green foliage,
shadows drawing long,

abstract possibilities,
symbols exciting
in their ancient newness:
water, snow, circles,
branches bare of birds

Statuary Sequence
for Keely Record

four-foot flamingo
rusting at the seams
dances with nature
beside butterflies
big as barn owls

                                       cement cat in spring garden
                                       —always sad

two concrete children,
arms crossed, tilted
into the same tree, counting
an eternal game
of hide-and-seek

                                       stone squirrel
                                       with prayer-clasped paws
                                       —above, acorns ripen

angels, saints, the virgin
Mary, and Jesus himself,
with backs turned, casting
the first shadows
—long, deep, dark

Sentinel Sequence

I

Morning haze
shrouds Henryetta hills
—trees have shed themselves
of their red rustling leaf-
pelts, now lying loam-soft

Red-tailed hawk
sits atop pole-fence arch,
its talons draw blood

-rust out of cracked-paint veins

II

White-wash rain
blots OKC full out
of existence all
at once—only tail lights
left floating on flood-roads

White pickup,
hydroplaned, faces down
traffic in red-blue

glow offering safety

III

Last day dregs
leak under wallcloud, light up
Mt Scott shell looming
above twinkling water
of Lawtonka lake town

Gas flare burns
lonely, an outpost in

tall-grass of prairie

—mist turns gold to shadow

IV

Refinery
lamps climb toward heaven
through the night—river
flow chops and breaks echoes
into brilliant billions

Opposite,
Tulsa skyline looks down
and winks itself out

—the night becomes itself

Oklahoma Skaibun

Oklahoma is obsessed with the sky, and fair enough. After all, it's the plain we're most known for, greater than any grassland, kept cleaner, clearer, than any windswept wheat field by far.

> mountain shouts in stone
> spires overshadowed by cloud
> —cotton-silent sky

'Course that same wind, sky, can turn nightmares into terrible reality real quick, quiet a least-peaceful prelude to tornadoes funneling from the firmament to flatten farmhouse, forest, field, fringe of city or small town smooth. Even before we'd been grouped in that most pertinent of geographical appellations (Tornado Alley), the sky had claimed more than we'd been willing to bargain when favorite sons Will and Wiley went down while overreaching the expanses of our own home atmosphere.

> early summer
> tornadoes no threat,
> but a promise
> —wind whippins
> raise us up right

But that hasn't stopped our obsession, hasn't kept us from counting seconds after lightning strikes to confirm the dark clouds just above are still fine. Nor has it peeled us from the front porch, peering through greening light at overhead whirlpools forming. In fact, we even named our only pro sports team after thunderbolts and thunderbirds, and we still boast our sky's the most open while we watch jets dice it into quadrants above kestrels and other kites cartwheeling through the blue.

> black slashes lighten
> into fall sky scars
> —contrails cauterized

        hawk hoops lazy-like
        through Sunday evening sunlight

And at night? Man, at night we'll sit hilltop for hours on end,
unbothered by the blinking of cell towers or satellites,
concentrating on the cosmos, drinking in the dazzle of other
planets' days.

            mid-summer hilltop:
            fireworks burst brilliant
            beneath even brighter stars

Part 2: Until Air Itself Is Tinted

The Trial of Paris
after Lucas Cranach the Elder

The true trial of Paris
was to see all the world
as beauty.
The wreaths
of flowers crowning, the stars
hung like ornaments
from the mountaintops,
and even the trees bestowed
with the same sensual curves
as the three bare-bellied
goddesses before him,

and he cursed to choose
but one most beautiful.

Among the Trees

This, a mighty red cedar
in a crease between two hills
grows large, green, bristling
against wind, rain, all elements
and erosions. It is solid,
everlasting. It
barely sways.

But when the lowest boughs
are penetrated, they reveal
not a single tree, but a copse
of cedars grown so close,
so intimate,
their branches strip each other vulnerable.

Each trunk creaks
in the breeze, leans
one into another.
The storm outside
can do no more
than swish an exterior
twig or two, for roots
run deep wrap tight,
strong as anchors holding
the whole world down.

A Winter Heat

The starting line was a finger
of hay meadow hill that reached
out and over the intersection
of a creek and its tributary.
The heat would pit an overturned grill
top (handle gone, of course)
against an oil drip pan stolen
from the local auto parts house.
At the call of "get set," both teams
took a head start, sprinting
into an almighty shove that sent
two boys lurching off over
the thin layer of snowfall.
The drip pan, slowed by the already
long blades of hay, came to rest
the usual 40 feet from the point of release.
The grill top, however, shot on,
furrowing through grass and gritty
snow with all the added momentum
a 165-pound 13-year-old boy can provide.
For him, the finish line was a row of bois
d' arc and red cedar, where he flung in,
screaming, beside a round bale that had
rolled-down-the-hill-and-into-the-creek-
all-on-its-own-we-swear and eventually
came up to a chorus of scratches and laughter.

The Screamer

It pendulums into
an outstretched smile
then up and over and
I'm reminded of Sallisaw,
a cage suspended, my
wallet slipping loose,
slapping the crossbar,
and me too scared to
reach for it, sliding off
and floating towards the
ground, the flaps catching
air like wings and spinning,
flinging loose a credit
card which slices off, just a
quick glint in the in-
candescent neon
glow of the upstart fair-
grounds that'd outgrown
the parking lot they'd
been birthed in.
                              This
memory the first ride upside
down I'd done deliberately,
stemming into more cages,
higher angles from which
to face the ground, head-
rushed and bloodmoved
and eyes watering, drops
falling, glinting sunlight,
plummeting soft like a body
that's overgrown its birth
and trusted gravity and
loose restraints over and over,
again, again,
                    to give that
          feeling of near-
death our species so desires.

Overlooking Freeny

Toy Story clouds drift
over a John Wayne valley
where treetops spike
and brown in glare of sun
some 5 years now after
having been stripped clean
of leaves by tornadoes
that pushed hilltop folk
underground, and on a clear day
you can see Caney, Atoka, Lane
radio towers blinking, dispelling
waves like the heat that ripples
off gravel driveway and hazes
a picturesque cow under horse
-apple bois d' arc branch and thorns
stabbing out like a lone tree
shining pretty on a hill.

Dandelion Morning

I linger at your graves like a crow,
a blossom of dark in the unreal light
of Sunday rising.

I don't know your names,
nor do my parents, grandparents,
your stones unmarked long before
they would even think of writing theirs.

But blood must be thicker than memory.

I'm sure we shared much—a face, perhaps,
an eye or two, a wide sense of humor.
Certainly a home. The family's
only owned so much land, stole
everything we had on the way into settling,
never looking anywhere but west and oh so wild.

Surely you sat the same hilltop I have,
saw the same stretch of Freeny Valley
fall off the face of God's greenest.

Did you notice, I hope?

Did it take the same 20 years
for it to be breath-taking,
or were you right away in awe?

Did you know the name
of the Milky Way arm
that reached above you,
so bright as to make night day?

Was it you poached the ponds dry
of anything but smallest perch
and muddy water?

Or perhaps you lined your pockets
and our creekbeds with red cedar,
windbreakers brought in to pollinize
the Bible Belt
with Christmas trees.

I don't know,
will never know,
how much of my world you built, shaped, shared.
Some would say all of it.

Still, I don't mind asking,
nor making the trip to Gethsemane
with a garden of my own—wildflowers:
bluebonnets, blankets, paintbrushes, primrose.
Oh, and dandelions.

All an attempt, small as it may be,
at marking the stones of the unknown.

Descending the Staircase

I

Perhaps time is relative,
related firstly to its keepers,
      those brothers bothered with worry,
      we watchers of mortal clocks

Who look to make our place
in the recording, voice our eternal
echoes and tick, tock, tap time
for our creations, capture each second,
      choosing theory over practice,
      intellect over tangible.

But for most, time is hardly dimension,
      no refraction of movement,
      but a reflection on moments.

Like a creek, they wade in it as it flows,
weighed down a little, softened should they stumble,
but thinking on it not, they see
their image in the ripples
in a mirror never twice the same,
but always recognized,
      fluid but whole,
      solid but changing.

II

Earlier (I suppose) I waited for a train stalled
on the track, considering how this engine,
once heralded as the dawn
of Industrialism and pragmatic metals,
      once the key to connections
      across countries and continents,

Today, serves as the easel for railyard Rembrandts
and divider of cities, classes, neighbors, friends, relatives.
      Making miles
      out of a single block,

I took the long way dirt road home
and found dust and light hanging
in thick curtains from green foliage,
      a picture frozen in space-time,
      an inspiration I'm glad I waited for.

Back home, the tracks had cleared.
      The train moved when I moved.

Hello Again, Green

trees of leafy expanse

moss of down
       -laid branch

grass shoots dangling
       from mouth of deer in dead sprint

poison ivy leaf, with oil-burnt
       holes in tri-pattern

youth in summer
       sun splashing

Sprite bottle, bobbing along
       in his wake

snake-doctor, saddling up
       the slithering heel-biter

lichen, expanding
       across stone overlooking

oily film in stagnant pool stocked
       with detritus of living

needles, littering the floor
       beneath straight-armed pine

horse-apple, here,
       miles from any bois d' arc bough

turtle, popping under
       soft shell of rippling

water, thick with itself and
       slow, and hiding

fish, whose mouths
        gulp an air fresh and cool like

evening, the first in months
        the heat of humanity has not overcome

your balming shade and driven all life indoors
        to sweat

all the same.

Li Po

Legend has it Li Po drowned
embracing the moon in the river—
little did he know,

he could have held a sea of stars
had he only waited 'til morning.

Not Crippled but Broken
after David Bates

You'd think with all the water
the world would soften some, yet
here are trees stabbing the sky, hard
corners of homes not crippled but broken
all the same, and now the flood
becomes the asphalt road you walk
your way out on, carrying sacks of solid waste
because it's all you could save, but nothing,
nothing, could be as hard as your gaze.

Another Night in Paradise

Walking in twilight,
the spiders
creep up on
front lawns saturated
from two days' rain.

Surrounded by arachnoid
benches, playsets, trampolines,
I am not afraid,
am plugged in, pink, at peace.

Even after oncoming headlights
hitch slight, then re-correct,
I am still
as the ditch water
I would have died in.

On the Valero Refinery on Veteran's Boulevard

There's a cloud factory in Ardmore
billowing columns
of combustible atmosphere
from steam punk colossi, which,
by day, bleed out
rust and grime and grease,
by night, spout
stars beneath the sky
so bright you forget
those finite twinkles
are mere facsimiles
of a blotted-out infinity.

Until Air Itself Is Tinted

As I await the redding hour
when Oklahoma sky forgets
its knotted white of cloud in blue
to paint all things in blood instead,

this moment lingers, stretching out,
like these last, longest rays of gold
stream steady, solid, at what surrounds
so as to soften hardest stone

and brick; they so illuminate
that on receding, all does not
so much cast shadows as absorb
to deepen, darken every spot.

Mimesis

He is captivated,
captures snapshots
of reflections in
creek water or
polished tile.

There, the world
glosses smooth,
sectionalized. It
cannot expand
forever, framed
by riverbanks
and baseboards
and borders of
pictures taken.
It is controlled,
shows only what is.
No one expects
anything more from it.

It must be nice,
he thinks, to live
in reflections,
where nothing is
quite as definite, and only
the lightest parts
of life happen.

And Back Again
after Jen Ninnis

The dream comes back to you,
as it does to all of us,
again and again and
you wake for it
again and again and
you lose so much sleep,
so   much   sleep,

so you act on it.

You try to go without,
dress yourself to the greens
and garbs of your surroundings, hoping
that oneness will find you
and be enough,
but you've too much
of your own color to not be
appreciated, and besides,
starfish do not fly like boomerangs,
and there is little other company here
where waves smash themselves
into a fine mist.

Perhaps this time you will find love
with someone complimentary, dull
enough to read notes
saturated by seawater,
or at the very least a bottle
without cracked glass or porous cork.

But, alas,
this is not your morning,
for your last hope has floated back

again.

For a Lover, at Dusk
after Rumi

Oh beautiful one,
let my love drift down
like twilight in the garden,
when darkness falls in fistfuls,
softening the edges of perception,
and all things true
become undone.

Revision, June 27

Night drops on this town
like dirt at a funeral:
a few fistfuls at first,
then shoveled in and
stamped down flat. But
weep not, for in the grave
like stillness, moth shadows
dance across wood slats
to the creak of porch swing
music while iced tea sweats
starshine onto work-worn palms.

Knee Deep in October

And what did I learn, wading
       the river in cool fall evening?
What, after wandering down worn sandstone steps?
       What, while tracing Tishominko's trails?

I learned of sand, sharp with shell and gravel,
       of rocks, smooth and grey and gorgeous,
and I learned the green of fall that drips
       from vines and branches and collects
as algae in pools where caves sprout from under dead logs.

As fresh-fallen dam water pushed each footfall
       further sideways, I wanted it to make meaning,
to be a metaphor for me and my work and the rushing
       of time like leaves on the wind or twigs in the water.

But it was just a river—a creek, actually—and even then
       too wide and winding to mind my wishes.

Learning to Lean

In Oklahoma, you learn
to lean into the blow
-ing wind like the last lover
you'll ever know,

and you're taught
to sleep with a fan on
not because you're hot,
but because you can't
trust the weather enough to sleep
with open windows, yet

when the wind leaves
no bedside to crawl into,
your skin learns to crawl

in the absence.

Joke

Clouds curl downward
like cat claws
kneading the earth

or goatees
tugged to the ground
by gravity

or some other
asinine animal analogy
to distract from the obvious

joke:
Only in Oklahoma
do clouds dream of being
tornadoes.

A Mild One

An ocean rolls in
above us, roiling,
the sky bifurcating
into after and

Before, all is dark
anxiety, the weight
of tons of water
waiting, static
building, preparing
to vaporize

Us, huddled under
roofs, the ground itself,
some closeted in
claustrophobia
of no loved
hands to hold.

Now, the break comes
a flood, the bottom
falling out and

Now, the wind and
rock unloosed and
you have no choice

Now but to ride it out
in silence, listening
for the earthshattering

Silence.

After, rain falls soft
through sunlight, and
as we sweep away

the shrapnel,
ice and stone,

We thank God
that we got off
so easy,
that we got out
at all.

Meditation

The leather magnolia
petals fall hard
as if to crack
the sidewalk, then lie
bowl-still beside
waxy leaves
already yellowed
by spring downshifting
into summer.

They twitch and skitter
like the bottlebrush tail
of a nearby fox squirrel,
lifted by the slightest
breeze to be thrown
a-ground anew. But

the petals hold,
brown in the sun,
and wait to catch
a rain that will make
all things green
once more.

University Boulevard

Drive by and look at
stately, self-important windows,
sterile symmetry,
stratified, red-brick walls.
Watch as it exhales
people from within, leaving
leafy sidewalks, lawns
sloping to and from,
with waxy green tree and grass
blades and maybe blooms
blossom over underneath
red-peeling benches.
Brilliant, illuminating
orbs where needed to
light ways to outside,
find spaces out and way out,
diasporic in daylight,
at night become
penultimate penumbra
parking lots and lots
of long walk, loneliness cars
on the outer curb.
Keep going, outside, outside
Now, (be serious)
now, look left to Spanish church
where workers, prostrate,
rest like the dead from rooftop
maintenance above
blue-stained glass images of
your god (is their god also,
just a different tint).

Visions of Durant, OK

who loned it through the streets in Idaho seeking visionary indian
angels who were visionary indian angels
—Allen Ginsberg, "Howl"

I saw him today, Allen.

Saw him as I blew
down Enterprise Boulevard
like an eastern wind.
Saw him framed above
the road in the unbroken
but backlit clouds.
Saw him in ragged blue jeans,
work boots, neon green
construction tee shirt, and smudge
of white helmet with
Choctaw Nation stamp.

Saw him with two great crane necks
rising up behind, sprouting
from his back like wing
spine mast poles waiting
to unfurl, pressing
the sky higher and higher
on hydraulic pistons,
freeing us to breathe and fly
and stoop no more.
Saw him like a new Coyote
trickster god, polycultural,
polyperson, vertex
of tribe and industry, holding
cedar sapling with one palm
and backhoe at bay
with another.
Saw him like titan Atlas,
with raw shoulders, standing tall
on muddy mountain spine of Mother Earth.

Saw him later, hopscotching
railroad ties, just this side
of Arkansas in bleak light,
trafficky, kicking gravel
in flip-flops in dead winter.
Saw him with gothic trees
snaking up behind
to screen silhouette
of smokestack steeple.
Saw him with cigarette, puff-puffing
like the engine he watched screech
away, wondered what
he wondered while he wandered,
he in undershirt and sweats,
with mustache penciled,
too dark to mark his complexion.

Saw him on 7th, too, on
asphalt parking lot,
dancing in technicolor
costumes to Spanish music.
Saw him as many
children, circling up, holding hands,
dancing, singing, rehearsing.

Saw the both of him
hugging, being hugged
out on the front porch,
twisting high on Conversed toes,
blue jeaned and sweatered,
star-ankled and starry eyed
behind glasses over a shoulder
and around the dark
hood of a brother,
prodigal perhaps,
or always there and loved
just the same.

Saw her squeeze
her smile into his

chest, under long hair,
peeking at the road, at who
might be watching, daring them,
daring all of us,
to say or to love
anything this much,
this sure, this certain.

I saw him, Allen,
saw the visionary indian
angel that you sought.
I saw him, and he was everything
you never promised
and nothing more,
        but nothing less, too.

**A Grasshopper Rode My Passenger Side Mirror
from Sonic, Down 2nd Towards the Aldridge Bldg,
By the First Drive-Through Bank in Oklahoma
(No, the Bank First Oklahoma Drive-Through,
My Bad) and the Rainbow Buffalo Bike Rack,
Right at the Charcuterie Place with the Lending
Library that has Mark Twain Graffitied on It,
Left at the Bearded Barbershop, Right Again
at the Gas Station on Carl Albert, Across the Bridge
Over the Old Ironworks, Between the Walgreens
and CVS Sat Catty-Cornered, Past the Hospital
Complex Beside the Cemetery, and All the Way
to Campus**

at no point
was he any
closer
than he appeared

Just Before the Rain-Out

for Ron Wallace

Black clouds slide in,
stain the skyscape smoky
like the whole world
east of us is burning
in the wake of sun rays
and dry lightning, but

kids keep on swinging bats,
keep on driving baseballs
back, back, back west
into what's left
of a nothing-but-blue afternoon,

racing the sun to the setting,
trying to knock it out of the sky.

Sun Showers

August first
and already
oak leaves
are half into
browning,
the remainder
wrinkling
yellow like
grasses below
baked golden.

Still, dust
puffs form
over gravel
drive, weave
through drop
lines catching
light while
wind shakes
lesser rain
storms loose
from hackberry
limbs.

Along
the lane,
families
under eaves
witness this
first fall
in many weeks
of summer,
this dog day
dawning rain
-drenched, each
person a plot

of parched earth
soaking in
the scene.

Disillusionment of 10:30

after Wallace Stevens

The inside is darker
than the outside,
but even lacking
stiff sunlight and heat,
the shadows draw long
and threaten fever.

There are no people,
is no person.
A cricket creeps past
as loneliness
lounges on the sofa,
dozes beneath
the spider spinning
a sharp ceiling corner
cushioned.

A cloud
breathes the world
out of being.

In Words and Trees
for Randy Prus

I

Four poems in
and I can hear you breathing
pure particulars, perceiving
the world atomized
then recollected,
crystalline—still

simple images with ill-defined borders.

II

Three squirrels thrash
through the lowest magnolia branches,
three more groundside eye me
expectant, but not afraid,
then dart below bushes

—likewise, leaves fall and flit in silence.

Pastures of Plenty

Light cuts golden across
this mountain meadow,
the burning west weaving
straight shadow out of an
Eastern Kingbird sat surveying
his subjects. Whole herds
of cattle, some hundred head,
graze alongside the same
count of deer, does
close enough to the road
you'd think they've never
known a human or hunter.

Such blithe innocence
is so much I forget
I've driven myself lost,
and instead I find myself
giving thanks that the world
still lets us do so
every now and again,
lest we miss pastures
plenty in pursuit of
golder ones.

Lost Lake

Littered
with lily
pads less
the blooms
but still
a steep
oak leans
over for
a better
look
its leaves
adding
with each
wind-ripple
shimmering
circlets
of green.

Meanwhile
fishing line
flosses
blackjack
and brush
along the
grinning
bank
bark rolls
like smoke
-paper
ash dust
dirt swept
clean
of campsite
mix with loam
of maple
trees
fall-dropping
great

splotches
of red pink
yellow
brown
orange
for me
to shamble
on lost
but liking
what I see.

October Rain

comes tripping down
the tin-top curling
like quotation
marks underneath
these "eaves."

I walk wet morning
as whitetail like light
mist traipse the
dawn graze dew
-drunk grass
crawdads raise
rain-glazed claws
praise pregnant
skies and water
flows all at once.

A sheet of puddle
slides over
pavement congeals
into solid soft and
slips across the
threshold
into a storm drain.

Droplets large
as thumbs sound
the darkness.

These Branching Moments

Why worry
for forks
in time,
for effects, yields,
effects, yields,
etc.?

Is not
each new
experience
an adventure,
the unknown
made manifest
as lessons learned?

What branch is not
fit for perching?
What wood won't
work for burning?

Even the thinnest twig
can leaf or bud up
and burst out blooms.

And upon falling?
Petals and leaves
whisper along asphalt
or pile pretty
for playing children.

Meaningless Harmonies
after Hank Jones

What sound is the shape
of beauty?

              Surely chimes
have something to do with it.

The click and shush
of ceiling fans is more
"comfortable,"
             the creak
of floorboards and rust-
chained swings too shadowy.

The acoustics of a morning
shower are marvelous, but
I'd hardly call my own voice
"beautiful."

Perhaps an evening
wind leafing through the trees
like a library full enough to fix
the future,
             or the silence
of a cat critic, lazing across
a poem to be?

           This repose
the only proper response,
given that meaning matters
less than the moment captured,
the writing of the reader
into experience,

the lines
of the poem like music staffs,
dissolving into nothing

but sound and beauty.

Variations at Night

I

At night, the pigs
seep into the divots
they spent all day
digging, meanwhile
pine trees glow orange
and won't tell me why.

In all the silence, lob
-lollies burst into being
like the explosion
of each needle-bunch,
each pinecone a grenade
glowing also, and also
saying nothing.

Great clouds witness all,
diffuse light into what
passes for smoke
and mystery beneath
the never-ending
that engulfs and expands
always, yet takes
the time to peer
into a lonely pasture
where pink stubbled
black-brown burrows
into sleep.

II

At night, the house
cools quickly under
roof strung with hung
-air circles and chains
wiggling like worms
while the ceiling creaks

itself quiet.
                Sounds like
a hair comb stood up
and run teeth-ways
along counter-spines
pop and bend through the dark.

The night, too,
resounds
in all its breathing.

III

At night, the distance
stutters, confused
as to who is where,
with whom, and how
they got there
                in the dark
your hand in mine is done,
no words needed.

We of one mind
think the thing then
the body reacts
                funny,
I'd not noticed before
that thought
                might mean action.

The body responding
                        surely
something must spawn first.

Forgive me, I've wandered
from you, from the point
I was thinking
                of you
I was thinking

                         so close
            seemingly
sandwiched

but no.

Turtle Island Sticky Note

Found:
sticky note
torn halfway
through
those lovely
memories

now a bookmark
teasing forever
text saying
Sorry
this isn't longer
but I'll write you
later!

       I do not
know Kim but
I keep her
love
       stuck
between
my favorite
poems
       and hope
she will make good
on her promise.

Orchid

after ee cummings

Or
ch
id in
a va
se, so sl
end
er, d
elica
te, ta
lling, gree
n, pin
k lea
ves vas
t as t
he win
ter thr
ough t
he win
dow w
hat mak
es t
he who
le ho
use su
rroun
ding you
so co
ld.

Fog Like Flame

Fog like flame
lights evening
streets in orange,

burning this city
to the ground
til dew settles
as ash,

soft and dark.

Snowmelt

How quickly
we forget
our wonder.

How soon
after sleep
we lose
the dream.

These crystals
become drops
of water

just the same.

After the Solstice

Blow gentle, friend,
just enough to lift the gray
from the embers.

Stir the coals
as best you can,
but be patient, know
that no fire builds
in but a moment,

that there is no promise
this hearth will relight,
but its history of heat
has earned it
another chance.

If there is any strength
still in these logs, let them
give it, let them lick light
and warmth into the corners
of the room the way
the morning sky, even after
the darkest night, glows
red along the edges
then flickers into full orange
blaze above trees of snow,

rekindling all that is good
in the cinders of yesterday.

Tonight

I took a walk tonight
before the metaphors came out.

The birds were just birds,
the wheelbarrows only wheelbarrows,

And this despite a blue, deep sky
and twilight's redding cloud.

Notes on the Poems

In order of appearance:

"A Work in Progress" refers to Jeanetta Calhoun Mish's collection of poetry, *Work is Love Made Visible* (West End Press, 2009).

"An Introduction" includes an excerpt from a poem formerly published by the author. The italicized portions are lines from a haiku first published by the journal *Frogpond*, then collected in the author's chapbook, *Among the Trees* (Fine Dog Press, 2021).

"chickadee tanka" is an ekphrastic piece responding to Bryan Dahlvang's *Chickadee*, which the author encountered via the Oklahoma Visual Arts Coalition's traveling exhibition 24 Works on Paper (2020-2022).

"String Sequence" is an ekphrastic piece responding to Irmgard Geul's *The Forest I Remember*, which the author encountered via the Oklahoma Visual Arts Coalition's traveling exhibition 24 Works on Paper (2020-2022). Geul's work was a multimedia piece incorporating string art.

"Statuary Sequence" is a series of tanka and haiku inspired by Keely Record's yard art tanka series.

"The Trial of Paris" is an ekphrastic piece responding to Lucas Cranach the Elder's *The Judgement of Paris* (Germany, c. 1528).

"Overlooking Freeny" and "Dandelion Morning" both refer to Freeny Valley, an area just northeast of the author's hometown, Caddo, OK.

"Descending the Staircase" is titled after Marcel Duchamp's *Nude Descending a Staircase, No. 2* (France, 1912).

"Not Crippled but Broken" is an ekphrastic piece responding to David Bate's *The Deluge II* (USA, c. 2007). The painting is part of his series on Hurricane Katrina.

"And Back Again" is an ekphrastic piece responding to Jen Ninnis' *Message in a Bottle* (USA, c. 2018), which the author encountered via *Rattle* poetry's May 2018 Ekphrastic Challenge.

"University Boulevard" is named after a street in the author's college town, Durant, OK.

"A Grasshopper" makes many references to downtown businesses and landmarks in McAlester, OK.

"Lost Lake" refers to an area of Robbers Cave State Park in Wilburton, OK.

"Turtle Island Sticky Note" makes reference to Gary Snyder's collection of poetry, *Turtle Island* (New Directions, 1974). The poem incorporates found poem elements, as the italicized portions were found handwritten on a sticky note lodged within the author's copy of the collection (bought used).

Acknowledgments

Many thanks to the editors, staff, and readers of the following journals, websites, and anthologies which first published some of the poems in this collection:

Atlas Poetica 40
The Bamboo Hut
Dragon Poet Review
Frogpond
Ninth Letter
Poem Journal
Red River Review
Voices

"Knee Deep in October" has been collected in the anthology *Level Land: Poems for and about the I35 Corridor* (Lamar University Press, 2022).

"Revision, June 27" and "A Grasshopper" were both selected to be displayed in the Rural Oklahoma Museum of Poetry's "Okla-Poet-Homa" exhibition from April to December of 2023.

"Lost Lake" and "Graveyard of Geese" appear in *The Oklahoma Review*.

Also, many of the poems collected here were first published in my chapbook, *Among the Trees* (Fine Dog Press, 2021), including: "In Morning," "Bird Watching," "Statuary Sequence," "Among the Trees," "Hello Again, Green," "Mimesis," "Revision, June 27," "Knee Deep in October," "Meditation," "University Boulevard," "Visions of Durant, OK," and several haiku selections from "Bird Seed Haiku."

Finally, my thanks to the members of the Oklahoma writing community, without whom I would find little joy in poetry, and especially to:

Jeanetta Calhoun Mish and the various faculty and students of Oklahoma City University's Red Earth Creative Writing MFA program, where many of these poems were written and edited.

Ken Hada and all the organizers and artists involved in the Scissortail Creative Writing Festival, where many of these poems have been read.

Ron Wallace, who has graciously allowed me to co-host *Poetry on Lost Street* in Durant, OK, since its inception.

The many members of the McAlester Public Library Poetry Club and Latimer County Arts Council, for allowing me to not only join in their writing, but to assist in organizing events.

Finally, Paul Bowers of Turning Plow Press, for all of his efforts in editing this manuscript, and for his unwavering support of the Oklahoma writing community.

About the Author

Photo Credit: Sherri Whisenhunt

Cullen Whisenhunt is a graduate of Oklahoma City University's Red Earth Creative Writing MFA program. He lives and writes in southeastern Oklahoma and has taught English for Southeastern Oklahoma State University and Murray State College. He currently teaches at Eastern Oklahoma State College in McAlester, OK, where he helps organize writing events with local libraries and writing clubs. He also co-hosts a monthly reading series in Durant, OK, and is a contributing editor for *Archive Serendipities,* where he discusses early Oklahoma poetry. He has published two chapbooks of poetry with Fine Dog Press: *Among the Trees* (2021) and *Childish Thing and Other Experiments* (2023).